Barnsley Buses

BARNSLEY BUSES

STEPHEN FARNSWORTH
and
ROGER GLISTER

Wharncliffe Books

First Published in 2001 by
Wharncliffe Books
an imprint of
Pen and Sword Books Limited,
47 Church Street, Barnsley,
South Yorkshire. S70 2AS

For up-to-date information on other titles produced under the Wharncliffe imprint, please telephone or write to:

Wharncliffe Books
FREEPOST
47 Church Street
Barnsley
South Yorkshire S70 2BR
Telephone (24 hours): 01226 - 734555

ISBN: 1-871647-91-6

A CIP catalogue record of this book is available from the British Library

Cover illustration: *A Northern Counties bodied Leyland Tiger PS2/5 entered service in 1962 and retired in 1973*

Printed in the United Kingdom by
CPI UK

Contents

Introduction

It was with considerable pleasure that I accepted the commission to compile this book from the wonderful collection of photographs that Stephen Farnsworth had in his possession. He has spent a large part of his life putting together this detailed pictorial history of the Yorkshire Traction Company that has fascinated him since childhood.

I, too, have known this company all my life and travelled many thousands of miles on their buses. Being brought up in Sprotborough, it was the Yorkshire Traction that we used to go to Doncaster on a regular basis. I remember very well walking along Station Road and passing the old Grand Theatre on my way to catch a number 49 bus back home. In the early 1950s, this theatre was almost a house of ill repute - their variety shows included young ladies *déshabille* and I was always rushed past the display boards lest my young mind be corrupted.

Upon attending school in Mexborough, the school buses were supplied by Yorkshire Traction and I can recall the excitement when the first 'flat fronter' was used on the school run. If one was kept in after class and missed the school bus, the walk to the West Street terminus in 'down-town' Mexborough to catch a service bus was quite an adventure for a twelve-year-old lad on a dark winter's evening.

Whereas I only knew two bus routes intimately, Stephen knew them all. Besides travelling all the local runs from Barnsley as, at first, a conductor and then as a driver, at weekends he would take charter trips to Blackpool or Scarborough. In fact he could not get enough of the Yorkshire Traction Company. His dedication is ably demonstrated through this extensive collection which he now shares with us all.

Roger Glister, March 2001.

About the Authors

Stephen Eric Farnsworth was born in January 1959 and brought up in his parents' home in Barnsley.

The son of a former development mining engineer he developed an interest in the Yorkshire Traction Bus Company at an early age and started amassing his extensive collection of photographs.

Educated at the Oaks Secondary Modern School in Kendray, Stephen joined Downings Steel as an apprentice plater welder after leaving school in 1975. He realised a long held ambition by going to work as a conductor with Yorkshire Traction in October 1976. Following a break with the company in 1976. Stephen returned as a trainee driver in September 1983. In 1987 he formed his own car audio and security firm and is presently involved in the leisure industry.

During his career at Yorkshire Traction, Stephen collected many hundreds of photographs of all the fleet vehicles together with all property owned by the company. He also recorded the changing face of Barnsley town centre and photographed much ecclesiastical architecture around the Barnsley area.

Roger Glister was born and bred in Sprotborough, a village to the east of Doncaster, where his early memories of the Sheffield and South Yorkshire Canal provided a basis for his lifelong interest in historic transport.

Educated at Mexborough Grammar School and Doncaster College of Technology, Roger has written extensively on the history of all types of transport with an emphasis on Inland Waterways. A long standing member of the Vintage Sports Car Club, Roger campaigns enthusiastically in his 1930 MG.

He is a professional engineer and designs heating systems for churches in the York and Leeds & Ripon Diocese.

The Yorkshire Traction Bus Company

November 1902 heralded the birth of mechanical public transport in Barnsley when the first tramcar service ran on the fledgling network. The enterprise was operated by the 'Barnsley and District Electric Traction Company' which, in turn, was a subsidiary of the 'British Electric Traction Company' (B.E.T.). This company, set up in 1895, promoted new tramway schemes throughout the land which were subsequently sold on to a locally promoted company; in this case the 'Barnsley and District Electric Traction Company'.

Ten tramcars were operated in the first instance from the new depot in Sheffield Road to five termini at Hoyland Common, Smithies, Locke Park, Ardsley and Dodworth Road. The inaugural runs were greeted with much acclaim and the vehicles were kept very busy throughout the day. The last tram to be put into service was purchased from the Brush Company in 1912 and brought the total of vehicles to fourteen.

With the rapid development of the motorbus and its freedom of travel, not encumbered by tracks or overhead power supply, the days of expansion of the tramway network in Barnsley were numbered. Buses had been running on routes mainly unsuitable for tramcars since 1908, but on 31 August 1930, all the ageing tramcars were replaced by Leyland Titan double deck buses.

It was in January 1929, following an Extraordinary General Meeting on the 12 November 1928, when a resolution was brought into force to change the name of the Company to The Yorkshire Traction Company Limited. Back in 1919 the word 'Electric' had been dropped from the company's title to bring it more into line with the increasing number of motor buses being operated. The final change gave lie to the ever more ambitious aspirations of the company to extend its operations further and further afield beyond its native Barnsley.

By the late 1920s B.E.T. was running some 142 motor buses as well as the tramcars and had opened depots at Doncaster, Huddersfield and Mexborough in addition to the original at Sheffield Road. Contemporary advertisements proudly boasted that they served 164 towns and villages. A period of growth followed with the purchasing of no less than twenty smaller operators during a ten year period and the development of the long distance coach services from Yorkshire to Blackpool, London and Birmingham.

The demise of the tramways was seen in the 1930s. By now the trams were a very small part of the bus company's operations and in 1929/30 a bill was promoted in Parliament to permit the abandonment of the tramways and this was implemented on 1 September 1930 when the Lord Mayor of Barnsley drove the last tram into the depot.

With the outbreak of the Second World War in 1939, the fuel shortage hit the bus companies very hard and many services were curtailed or in many cases suspended. By 1940 the War Department were requisitioning all kinds of commercial vehicles and Yorkshire Traction did not escape the net. Twenty-two buses were taken and with no new replacements available, resources were stretched to breaking point. Makeshift repairs were the order of the day and such was the desperation to keep the fleet mobile that it was not unknown for broken crankshafts to be either bolted or welded back together.

Another austerity measure embraced by Yorkshire Traction was to run buses on 'produce' gas. The company had some twenty-nine vehicles converted to run on this fuel which was produced by burning coke on a small trailer towed along behind.

By the time of the armistice, the fleet was in a parlous state and rebuilding was undertaken as fast as the availability of parts and materials would permit. Every opportunity was taken to purchase any new vehicles that manufacturers could supply and expansion was once again the main aim. In 1952 the company celebrated its 50th anniversary with much increased service mileage and passenger levels had doubled from the pre-war numbers. Through to the mid-1950s, the growth continued until the Suez crisis of 1957 once again hit the fuel supplies. This time things did not improve as expected in the aftermath due to the rise in popularity of private motoring and passenger numbers stated to fall off in a dramatic fashion.

The gradual decline carried on for the next fifteen years and various economy measures were employed which enabled the company to keep its head above water until, in January 1969, it was absorbed into the National Bus Company. The following year saw Yorkshire Traction reach its maximum size when there were 398 vehicles operating from six depots.

In 1977 more than seventy-six million passenger journeys were made in a year and almost sixteen million miles were covered by the bus and coach services. The following pages of this book are a testament to the bus company that has been a household name in the West Riding of Yorkshire for almost seventy years and to one man's devotion to a unique collection of photographs that depict the changes wrought in the company and its environment over much of this time.

Roger Glister, March 2001

Chapter One

Makes and Types of Vehicles Used By Yorkshire Traction

This chapter shows the many and varied makers and coachbuilders engaged in the manufacturing of buses and coaches used by just one fleet operator. Most vehicles were purchased new but many arrived in service along with the smaller companies bought out by Yorkshire Traction over the years.

Purchased new in 1935, number 492 has had a very varied career and is still enjoying work today.

Starting life as a Roe bodied Leyland Tiger TS7 this vehicle entered service in April 1935 and carried on in this guise until, in 1950, a new body by Weymann was fitted. In 1958 after twenty three years of service 492 was withdrawn from the Yorkshire Traction fleet and sold to a building contractor as a workmen's bus. Some years later a travelling showman became the proud owner of the Leyland and eventually it ended up in an ignominious state as a caravan.

In 1980 Yorkshire Traction purchased 492 back again saving the bus from the wreckers. It was rebuilt from top to bottom and finished in the original 1935 livery with golden lettering.

Now a regular attender at vintage vehicle rallies, 492 is also popular for weddings and private functions. A remarkable achievement for a sixty-five year-old public service vehicle.

A Roe bodied Guy Arab 11 is pictured enroute between Barnsley and Doncaster. The driver would appear to have stopped on a road junction before leaving his cab. However, the passengers are still on board so the intention must be to carry on with the journey. The side advertisement is for 'Wimsol' the ubiquitous cleaner.

This is an unusual quartet of pictures that show three different buses from the same group in various stages of their careers. They are all 1947 Roe Bodied PS1 Leyland Tigers which served until 1958. AHE 788 looks to be still in service on the Doncaster route and to be in good condition. AHE 790 is displaying a 'Private' sign on the route indicator and appears to have seen better days. Further along the road to ruin is AHE 792 with fleet number 770. Derelict and vandalised, it awaits its fate parked up on some waste ground. Or, perhaps, a knight in shining armour came along and rescued it. The last picture shows 770 with the company name replaced with Mason & Nickelson resting in some coastal location. The eventual fate of this vehicle is unknown – can anyone help?

AHE 792

AHE 792

A workmen's special bus at the junction of Eldon Street and Queen's Road by May Day Green on the approach to Barnsley bus station. The vehicle is a Foden PVD6 with Willowbank coachwork and two stroke diesel engine purchased new in 1948 by W. A. Cawthorne and Sons. This firm was bought out by Yorkshire Traction in 1952 and the two vehicles that came with the deal being entered into service as fleet numbers 127 and 128. Number 127 was a 1938 Leyland Titan TT5. In the background to the left can be seen the Civic Hall on Eldon street and on the right is the area where the outdoor market stood. This is now replaced by the Barnsley Metropolitan Borough Council offices.

Fleet number 817 at Barnsley Bus Station with passengers embarking for the next service to Goldthorpe. The vehicle is a Leyland Tiger PS1 with Brush coachwork and was aquired by Yorkshire Traction in 1949 and retired in 1957.

Two PS1 Leyland Tigers with Brush bodywork that were taken into service in April 1949 along with twenty-six similar vehicles. Number 784 and 796, these two survived until 1956 in their original form; five others from the batch were re-built as double-deckers in 1956/7. Number 784 is proclaiming that 'Barnsley Brewery's Oakwell Ales' are 'Still the Best'.

The Huddersfield to Staincross service bus pictured in the early 1950's is fleet number 831. Purchased new in 1949 it is a Leyland Titan PD2/1 with Roe bodywork. 1962 saw the end of its life with Yorkshire Traction.

The lady passenger of number 1151 would seem to be assisting with the backing up of the vehicle whilst the conductor looks on! Seen in Barnsley this Leyland Atlantean PDR1/1 in the mid 1960's was new in 1959, was renumbered 600 in 1967 and was retired in 1975.

Seen in the centre of Wombwell this workmen's special is enroute to Mitchell Main colliery. A Guy Arab with Massey bodywork this double-decker entered service with Yorkshire Traction when new in 1943. Re-bodied by Roe in 1950 this vehicle carried until it was withdrawn in 1961. To the left can be seen the shop of the well respected Wombwell tailor, Fred Hadwen, long since departed. On the right are shops that later became the Prudential offices and are now occupied by a veterinary practice.

This Leyland Titan PD2/1 of 1950 is fitted with Roe bodywork and is seen at the Upper Sheffield Road depot. Bearing fleet number 882 this bus remained in service until 1962. It appears to be waiting for a crew to take it out on a tour of duty and, judging by the open upper windows, they have a fine, warm day for their journey.

Taken in the 1950's this picture shows the North Bridge in Doncaster with a Leyland Tiger PS1, fleet number 887, with Brush bodywork of 1950 heading out of town on its way to the old Fowler's factory at Sprotborough with a full compliment of work people for the next shift. During the Second World War this factory was turned over to the manufacture of armoured vehicles, becoming known locally as the Tank Factory until its eventual closure. Following the single-decker is another Leyland on route 49 which was to Sprotborough old village. The Doncaster North Bridge carries the A1, London to Edinburgh road, over the railway and the Sheffield and South Yorkshire Navigation canal and has been a major bottle-neck for most of the last century. It is only now, at the start of a new century, that the problem is being fully addressed and a relief road is being constructed from Bentley Road across the river, canal and railway and entering the town beyond St. George's Church by Greyfriars.

Fleet number 1098 is pictured in the yard outside the Yorkshire Traction Upper Sheffield Road Depot in the late 1950's. It is a Leyland Tiger Cub with a Willowbrook body supplied new in 1957 and was re-numbered as 432 in April 1967.

Another Leyland Tiger, number 888, consecutive with and identical to the bus on the previous page is seen on the Main Street in Sprotborough approaching the village green where the bus would stop in front of the village shop for a few minutes before returning to Doncaster Northern Bus Station. From the route indicator board, it would appear that the number scroll has been turned one digit short, as the correct number for the Sprotborough run was 49.

The workmen special is parked alongside OHE 712, a Willowbrook bodied Leyland Tiger Cub PSUC1/1, at Barnsley bus station. This behicle was in service from May 1959 until 1970 and was subsequently restored and preserved. Originally fleet number 473 it ended its working life as 1139. 783 is a Leyland Tiger

One of the first 'Flat Fronters' this Leyland Royal Tiger with Brush body is pictured in Waterdale, Doncaster. Displaying the early 1960's livery with front lettering being gold on a cream background panel. The advertising panel announces that 'Barnsley Brewery's Oakwell Ales' are 'Still the Best', and this is a sentiment shared by many thousands of people in South Yorkshire long after the untimely closure of the Oakwell Brewery. To the right can be seen the former Claybourns motor car showrooms, a long established Doncaster firm now sadly closed with the premises used by a furniture depot.

Fleet number 1192, a Leyland PS2/3 with Roe bodywork, started life in 1950 as fleet number 902 with a body by Windover and was rebuilt to its present form in 1960. Seen operating on route 66, 1192 is just leaving Sheffield city centre on its way back to Barnsley.

Pictured in Doncaster this Sentinal ST6 fleet number 130 with their own body was built in 1952 and aquired by Yorkshire Traction in January 1961 with the takeover of Camplejohn Brothers of Darfield. Looking very smart in what appears to be a fresh coat of paint, this photograph was possibly taken shortly after the takeover. Of the ten vehicles transferred only five were retained, fleet numbers 129 to 133 inclusive, being three Sentinals and two Atkinson Alphas, the remainder were sold straight on.

BHE 455, a 1949 Brush bodied Leyland Tiger PS1, is pictured in Waterdale bus station at Doncaster. The cafe seen on the extreme left served as the bus crew's canteen and was also the collection point for the small parcels delivery service carried out by most of the bus companies between the various bus stations.

Pictured in St. Sepulchre Gate, Doncaster is a 1951, Leyland Titan PD2/12 having arrived in the town from Barnsley. After passing Cantor's furniture shop it would shortly turn right past the old Postal Sorting Office into the railway station concourse where its journey ended. Behind the vehicle is Blaskey's wallpaper shop and further to the left can be seen the somewhat futuristic facade of the Doncaster Co-operative building. In the top left hand corner the overhead supply for the trolley buses can be seen.

A Leyland Tiger Cub PSUC1/1 of 1954 with Saunders Roe bodywork is parked in Doncaster bus station awaiting its turn of duty. Its route is number 50D to the small village of Burghwallis to the north of Doncaster. As fleet number 1019, this vehicle carried on until withdrawal in 1966.

This Leyland Tiger PS1 started life in early 1956 as a single-deck bus destined for work with County Motors (Lepton) Ltd of Huddersfield. However, before it could be delivered it was diverted to Yorkshire Traction and rebuilt as a double-decker by Roe and entered service in May 1956. Seen here in Barnsley at the foot of Market Hill, by the junction of Peel Square and Eldon Street, number 1072 is one of the last open back double-deckers to be in service in Barnsley. On the right can be seen Marks & Spencer's building that they still occupy today. On the left is the Barnsley branch of Burtons, the gentleman's tailor, which has long since disappeared from our high streets. Making use of the building today is one of the new style chain enterprises, Macdonalds. In the background, behind Burtons, are some of the old outdoor market stalls in Cheapside which have now been replaced by an indoor market complex.

Sheffield bus station is the location for this photograph depicting LHE 528, a Leyland Tiger Cub PSCU1/1 with Willowbrook body, carrying fleet number 434. Formerly numbered 1100 this bus served from June 1957 to 1970. To the left can be seen a Mini Minor and, quite a rarity, a Ford Consul Classic which dates the picture as the early 1960s.

Just returning from Worsborough Common this Guy Arab IV is pictured entering Barnsley bus station by the Queens Road and Kendray Street entrance. Built in 1958 for County Motors, 688 was transferred to Yorkshire Traction in January 1969, but its service with the new operator was short lived as it was withdrawn in August of the same year. Behind can be seen a Leyland Leopard with Plaxton Panorama coachwork waiting to carry a charter to Blackpool for the day. The archways forming the backdrop to this picture were built beneath the Court House railway station approach bridge and were used by different retailers as market trader's storage, shops and the bus station cafe.

A Leyland Titan PD3A/1 parked by the inspector's office at Barnsley bus station in the late 1960's. It is fitted with a Northern Counties body and entered service in 1961. If you were the last passenger to embark on this type of bus, you had to be very nimble as the air operated sliding door moved very quickly and was well known for trapping coat tails and, on occasions, feet. These Titans were the last buses with the isolated driver's cab to be used by Yorkshire Traction as the one man operated bus conception was already being introduced.

Seen leaving Doncaster North bus station VHE 203 is a Leyland Titan PD3/A which entered service in June 1961. Fitted with a Northern Counties body it was originally numbered 1203 but re-numbered 708 in June 1967. The advertisement on the bus side is urging people to stock up on cheap coal before the end of September when, presumably, the prices will rocket in time for the heating season!

Parked in tandem at Wombwell bus depot are VHE 206 and VHE 207 both of which are Burlingham bodied PSCU1/2T Leyland Tiger Cubs from April 1961. Originally with fleet numbers 1206 and 1207 they were re-numbered in 1967, 112 and 113 respectively. They were withdrawn in 1971.

Photographed in the late 1960's this Leyland Atlantean PDR1/1 with Weymann body was one of the first batch of the one man operation type of vehicle to operate in Barnsley and, indeed, anywhere in the country. Entering service in December 1959, with special low height roof to clear the low bridges encountered around South Yorkshire, 606 is seen approaching Queen Street on the way to the bus station. Originally numbered 1157 it was renumbered 606 in April 1967 and was eventually withdrawn in 1975.In the background to the left is the Civic Hall and the shops beneath with the premises of Albert Hurst, renowned throughout the land for his black pudding and pork pies that won him many awards. Next door was, and still is, the Barnsley branch of the Singer sewing machine company.

Seen in the overspill park at Barnsley bus station this Alexander bodied Leyland Tiger Cub PSUC1/2T entered service in April 1962 and survived until 1975, being re-numbered from 1214 in April 1967. Behind can be seen the Town Hall tower and the Queen's Hotel is once again prominent.

Pulling off Stand 11 at Barnsley bus station, this 1963 Willowbrook bodied Leyland Leopard PSU is heading for Blacker Hill. As can be seen, the Oakwell Brewery had a large advertising account with Yorkshire Traction, with both the bus and the bus station proclaiming the joys of Barnsley Bitter. Behind the bus and above the passenger's waiting room can be seen two of the station's time pieces, one analogue and the other digital.

Advertising Webster's Beers this Leyland Tiger PS2/5 is awaiting its driver before departing on route 99 to Rawmarsh. Rebuilt from Willowbrook bodied, Yorkshire Woolen District fleet number 706, this bus entered service with Yorkshire Traction in 1963 as number 1242 and was renumbered 793 in April 1967.

The church of St. Andrew overlooks a busy bus stage in the centre of Huddersfield in the last days of 1969. All three vehicles are Leyland Leopard PSU's with Willowbank bodywork and arrived at the Huddersfield depot of Yorkshire Traction on 1st January 1969 following the takeover of County Motors. It can be seen that the route number display area is blanked out, following County Motors practice, and the destination name board was relied upon for the necessary information.

Passing the Queen's Hotel on its right in Regent Street in the centre of Barnsley, a Roe bodied Leyland Titan PD3A/1 approaches the bus station having returned from Kexborough. This vehicle was purchased new in 1965 and enjoyed twelve years of service before being withdrawn in 1977. Yorkshire Traction ran two routes to Kexborough, one via Staincross along Eldon Street and the other, as covered by number 735, went by way of Barugh Green and Huddersfield Road.

Barnsley Town Hall tower can be seen in the background and a Morris Minor van is sandwiched between the two buses.

This scene is taken in the Pitfield parking area at Upper Sheffield Road in 1970. On the right is a Leyland Tiger PS2/5 with Northern Counties body. Following the arrival of the Atlanteans in the fleet these older Tigers would only be used as relief or for contract runs i.e. schools and works specials. On the left is fleet number 747, a Willowbrook bodied Leyland Atlantean PDR1A/1. Numbers 747 - 750 were diverted from Devon General to Yorkshire Traction in March 1969 and such was the urgency for them to be brought into service there was no time to repaint them, so they entered the fray in Devon General colours. The 'dropbox' route indicator can be seen to be black lettering on a white background, the opposite of Yorkshire Traction tradition.

Pictured in Park Street car park in Wombwell, Leyland Olympian, fleet number 651, waits to continue its travels on the Jump Circular route.

Number 223 is seen entering Leeds bus station sometime prior to December 1979 when it was re-numbered 123. It is a 1968 Leyland Leopard PSU3/4R with Alexander coachwork known as a 'semi coach' which was used initially for coastal services where it would pick up passengers en route and latterly for local motorway work. In their distinctive livery, red bottom half and white roof, these vehicles were also used for taking local organisations on their outings.

Shown travelling to the Manor Farm Estate in Rotherham, this 1970 Daimler Fleetline with two door Alexander body is an example of the model known affectionately as 'Jumbos' by their operators. Along with eight others, number 359 spent most of its working life at the Rawmarsh depot.

Taken in 1970, this photograph shows a 1969 Willowbrook bodied Leyland Atlantean PDR1A/1 leaving Barnsley bus station on the Athersley South Circular route. This was one of the routes operating the 'Drop Box' system in and around Barnsley. This system was designed to speed up the local services and was driver operated, whereby a cylindrical steel 'safe' was located at the side of the driver which had a clear perspex top with a coin slot through which passengers would place their fare. When the driver saw that the correct money had been deposited, an elbow operated lever dropped the coins into the 'safe' below. As no tickets were issued the system worked on trust throughout.

Looking very much unloved, this Alexander bodied Leyland Leopard PSU3B/4R has reached the end of the road. Entering service in 1971 as fleet number 237, it was renumbered 137 in 1979.

This sad picture shows part of the compound at the Wombwell Depot known as the 'Bones Yard' where all the withdrawn buses were stored. The central vehicle is an Atlantean consecutively numbered to the one in the previous photograph being number 748 and withdrawn in 1981 along with the rest of the batch 747 - 750. To the right is a Marshall bodied Leyland Leopard PSU4B/4R registration number CHE 533 K.

Fleet number 433 is a 1977 Leyland National 11351A/1R parked at Barnsley bus station. The pod to the rear of the roof housed the heating and ventilation units. This model also had the rear seats and floor raised to accommodate the engine underneath. The gentleman seen through the window is the 'whistler back', Mr. Alma Clayton, who would control reversing buses by means of blasts on his whistle. Vehicles had to reverse out of the stands into the traffic lanes unsighted which made the 'whistler back' a very busy man.

Fleet number 837, pictured in Kendray Street, is heading to Worsborough Common during the 75th year of Yorkshire Traction's existence. This Bristol VRT/SL3/501, new in 1976, sported a celebratory livery on its E.C.W. bodywork from June 1977 to July 1978 to commemorate the 75 years of service from 1902 to 1977. Unfortunately in 1981 this vehicle was badly damaged by fire and withdrawn from service.

Two very contrasting pictures of the same vehicle, a 1981 Leyland National Mk II fleet number 228, demonstrating the extremes of weather through which the buses must operate.

The 1985 winter scene is located on Honeywell Street approaching Old Mill Lane on the return journey from Rockingham Street to Barnsley bus station.

Seen in more clement weather, 228 is seen in Barnsley bus station outside the Y T C Travel Shop awaiting a further turn of duty. Numbers 228 & 229 were on trial with Yorkshire Traction having been fitted with fully automatic gear boxes. They did not prove popular and were soon sent packing!

Chapter Two

VARIOUS DEPOTS AND FACILITIES

This chapter shows various aspects of several Yorkshire Traction depots and in some cases the development over the years.

Upper Sheffield Road Depot at Barnsley was the nerve centre for the whole of the Yorkshire Traction undertaking since 1902. Pictured here in the mid 1950's the main offices can be seen to the right and part of the facade of the Pinder Oaks top garage.
The photographer's main subject for this picture is a Leyland Tiger Cub PSUC1/1 with Saunders Roe body when new in 1954.

Almost the same perspective as the previous picture but taken thirteen years later. The bus is, once again, a Leyland Tiger Cub but this time with a Park Royal body. The head office building to the right would appear to have had a face lift and looks much more cared for. On the facade of the garage can be seen the 'Depot Clock'. This timepiece was used by all crews leaving the depot for good time keeping.

The Pinder Oaks garage in all its glory as it was in 1983 and showing through the door to the right the garage staff mess room and the foreman's office. Just inside the door is an inspection pit used for day to day light repairs. Above the doorway can be seen the empty recess once occupied by the 'Depot Clock'. The bus is a Leyland National Mk.1 B52F of 1973 that was converted in the early 1980's to give wheelchair access which expanded even further the service offered by the Yorkshire Traction Company.

Another view of the Yorkshire Traction depot in Upper Sheffield Road showing, on the left, the entrance used by returning buses that have approached the depot by the service lanes. It was company policy that all vehicles would use this entrance to ensure they were refuelled after every trip, no matter how short the journey had been. To the right of the picture can be seen the Head Office entrance to the depot where all vehicles would exit onto the main road. In front of the garage is the Leyland National number 483, which was converted to serve the disabled people in the community. It was often to be seen parked outside Marks & Spencers in the Barnsley shopping precinct for the convenience of its passengers.

Yorkshire Traction head office seen in 1983 with the main entrance leading to the reception area. The General Manager's office is located on the upper floor at the front left hand corner, giving unrestricted views of the bus service lanes both entering and leaving the depot. This building also housed the cashier's office, the time office and the inspectors' office and the staff mess room. In the time office all the daily duty rosters were compiled. To the extreme left can be seen the gate leading to the traffic office, the training area and staff car park.

The road staff mess room at the head office building where all bus crew would collect their ticket machines, waybills and cashing in slips prior to going on duty. Through the window on the left is the cashing in office and to its left is a night safe for late turn crews to deposit their takings.

This pleasant building was converted from a detatched residence to form the traffic office and publicity department. To the right is a portacabin used by the training school and to the far left can be seen the Pinder Oaks garage. This building was demolished in the 1990's to create further car parking space.

All available space was put to useful purpose throughout the depot and this picture ably displays the ingenuity used. These garages, for the maintenance and storage of the smaller vehicles of the fleet, are built under the vehicle ramp in the Upper Sheffield Road depot. The mechanic responsible for the servicing or repair of the cars and vans kept in this workshop was also employed as a chauffeur to the chairman and managing director, driving the company's Jaguar.

The sub-depot at Rawmarsh where limited repairs and maintenance would be carried out. This depot operated a 'one way' vehicle system where buses entering the depot used the right hand entrance at the side of the workshops. They would proceed through the bus wash to the rear of the building for either re-fuelling or parking and when leaving would use the exit shown to the far left of the picture. Yorkshire Traction coach fleet number 1 can be seen to the right parked in the steam cleaning bay.

Pictured at the Rawmarsh Depot, fleet No. 1, a Plaxton bodied Leyland Leopard, is having its under body steam cleaned on the steam bay situated at the side of the workshops. It is in the combined livery of Yorkshire Traction and National Express and was used daily on services to Birmingham and London.

Showing the Shafton sub-depot with an Eastern Coachwork bodied Bristol VRT parked outside awaiting its turn on duty. Buses operating from this small depot ran services mainly in West Yorkshire. The ubiquitous square faced Yorkshire Traction time clock can be seen very clearly above the doorway. Inside this large building were housed all the ancillary offices and staff mess rooms.

Squashed in between the funeral director's chapel and the workshop building, the bus wash at Shafton was also the service lane for all buses re-fuelling when returning from service.

Seen at the Yorkshire Traction Wombwell Depot, fleet number 836, a Bristol VRT, is proudly displaying the winning entry in a 'Paint a Bus' competition run by the Barnsley Chronicle. 836 is standing outside the main workshop at Wombwell which also contained the depot offices and staff canteen. Part of the open ground at this depot was used to store disused or scrapped fleet vehicles and was known as the 'Bone Yard'.

Located at the side of the workshops at Wombwell is the bus wash and refuelling service lane. The diesel storage tanks are mounted on top of the bus wash with the delivery pipes running down the outside. The cylindrical water tank to the left fed the automatic bus washing apparatus. Upon entering the service lane all buses were obliged to stop and whilst re-fuelling was taking place, a defects slip had to be filled in and signed by all drivers. Any fault that could be handled 'on the spot' was dealt with but anything more serious the bus would be directed into the workshops or taken out of service.

Chapter Three

Coaches and Excursions

Coaches were a natural development of the service bus when bus companies realised that groups of people would pay good money to be transported, not just to the shops or to work, but for days out and excursions to romantic destinations previously only dreamed about. These buses were fitted with much more luxurious coachwork and better upholstered seats. In the case of the coach, the comfort of the passenger became paramount as a means of getting them back on the bus at weekends for a trip to Scarborough as well as every other day for the journey to work.

In service from 1951 to 1962, fleet number 927 is a Leyland Royal Tiger PSU1/15 with a Windover body. Photographed whilst parked up in Waterdale, Doncaster, the coach would probably have been running a coastal run for day trippers.

EMERGENCY DOOR

During the 1930s, bus tours were rapidly gaining popularity and the bus companies were keen to capitalise on this. The Yorkshire Traction 'Sun Saloon' was one such attempt and this promotional brochure was used to great effect in drumming up trade from clubs and associations for their coastal trips and annual outings. The interior view shows several points incorporated into the design of this purpose built coach. The large opening sunroof for those finer days can be clearly seen and the circular hot air blower that would have kept at least the first two rows of passengers warm on colder evenings. There are curtains for every window and ash trays for every seat. The luggage racks are designed in such a manner that, unless you read the little warning notice on the seat back, you will hit your head upon rising from your seat.

The Yorkshire Traction speciality was the Evening Circular Tour which travelled some fifty to sixty miles to the moors above Holmfirth or to North Derbyshire for a cost of 2s or 2s 6d (10p or 12½p) per passenger. In 1936 over 8,000 people took advantage of this service which ran each Sunday evening during the summer months.

Fleet number 872 would appear to have made a stop for ice creams enroute for Birmingham. The little girl on the front seat is enjoying hers whilst the driver is still absent. He may be in the left hand shop buying Wills 'Woodbines' or 'Cobnut' tobacco. This Windover bodied Dennis Lancet 111 entered service new in August 1949 and was retired in 1959.

Another refreshment stop! This time the driver seems to be asking a passer-by to get him a sandwich for his lunch. CHE 952 is an express coach built by Windover on a Leyland Tiger PS2/3 chassis in 1950. Retired in 1960 this vehicle was rebuilt by Northern Counties and re-entered service as THE 187 with fleet number 1187 and became 783 in 1967.

GHE 26 is a Willowbrook bodied Leyland Tiger Cub PSCU1/2 of 1954. Seen here travelling between Barnsley and Wakefield, number 1026 was finally retired from service in 1965.

This Atkinson Alpha was built by Plaxton in 1957 for Camplejohn Brothers of Darfield with fleet number 26. When this firm was taken over by Yorkshire Traction in January 1961, it was given the number 133 but lasted only five years before being withdrawn. It is seen here parked up having brought an excursion to Scarborough for the day.

Plaxton of Scarborough built this Leyland Tiger Cub coach in 1959 which is parked somewhere near Blackpool according to the destination board. Originally numbered 1145 it was re-numbered 107 in 1967 and retired in 1970.

Pictured in Holmfirth, this Marshall bodied Leyland Leopard PSU3/4R is an express coach to Manchester. Entering service in May 1967 it was withdrawn ten years later.

Fleet number 927 again, this time parked at Scarborough having brought a bus load of children from Ryhill. The coach had been chartered by the 'Ryhill Ex-servicemen's Club' who had sponsored the children's outing.

This Leyland Tiger Cub with Willowbrook body entered service in 1956 and ten years later was converted to handicap use having been transferred to Barnsley Borough Council, hence the Barnsley coat of arms on the front panel. It featured a wheelchair lift and had seating for twenty one persons. The bus was allowed parking and service facilities at the Upper Sheffield Road depot but was manned by council staff. It was finally taken out of service in 1969.

Acquired in 1964 when Yorkshire Traction took over W. Pickersgill of Low Valley, this Bedford SB5 with Duple body, fleet number 139, first entered service during 1962. The coach is seen here on charter for the Omnibus Society's Presidential Weekend, which would appear to be very well supported as a second Yorkshire Traction coach can be seen alongside.

Having just arrived at the Coliseum Coach Station, off Lytham Road, Blackpool, this Yorkshire Traction coach is unloading luggage and passengers for a holiday in Blackpool. Fleet number 2 is a Leyland Leopard PSU3/3RT, with Plaxton coachwork. When new in 1963, it was the 1000th Leyland bus to be delivered to the Yorkshire Traction company and had the honour for some time to carry this number beneath the maker's badge on the front panel. Re-numbered 2 in April 1967, it was finally retired in 1975. The Blackpool service ran daily, travelling through many towns and villages on the way and taking some five hours to complete the journey.

Fleet number 19 is a Duple bodied Leyland Leopard PSU3/3R which started life as number 108 with the Mexborough & Swinton bus company in 1965. Acquired in 1969 by Yorkshire Traction it was used in service until 1975. It is pictured here in the main bus station at Morecambe having just dropped off a full load of holiday makers. The driver can be seen to be wearing an early pattern summer uniform jacket, grey with red collar and cuffs, which was later phased out with the advent of the National Bus Company.

A Leyland Leopard PSU3/3R with Plaxton coachwork, this coach was originally numbered 1332 and was given the number 13 in April 1967. It was taken out of service in 1977. This type of vehicle would be used on coastal services, private hire contracts, school outings and, on occasions, scheduled services if there was a shortage of buses. It can be seen leaving the service lanes at Upper Sheffield Road depot at Barnsley.

Parked up at Barnsley bus station, fleet number 225 is an Alexander bodied Leyland Leopard PSU3A/4R. This type of semi-coach was used mainly for coastal service and stage carriage work on routes such as Sheffield or Manchester. New in 1969 and re-numbered 125 in December 1979 this vehicle was retired in 1980.

Fleet number 1131 seen in the mid 1960's at Barnsley bus station is a Leyland Tiger Cub PSUC1/1 of 1959 with the newly regulated 36ft. long, 54 seat body. It is finished in cream and red livery with gold lettering and was used extensively for private charter.

Seen at the rear of the Drill Hall on Eastgate in the centre of Barnsley, number 29 is a Leyland Leopard PSU3B/4R with Plaxton coachwork of 1973. This part of the Court House car park was used by Yorkshire Traction for the arrivals and departures of many of their coastal services. This coach was also kept busy transporting passengers to and from Cannon Hall Park at Cawthorne on the occasion of Queen Elizabeth's Jubilee Visit on the 12th July 1977.

Also parked in the Court House car park this 1978 Plaxton bodied Leyland Leopard PSU3E/4R is awaiting a run to London and return as part of the National Express service. By this time long distance coaches were beginning to incorporate a degree of luxury for their customers with reclining seats and window curtains. The Court House car park was convenient for use as a coach station and park due to the multiple access by Regent Street or Old Mill Lane thus avoiding inconvenience to other road users.

With the body-shop as a back-drop, a Plaxton bodied Leyland Leopard painted in 'Rapide' livery prepares to depart on route 560 to London. Number 52 was one of the first coaches obtained by Yorkshire Traction to be fitted with 'on board' entertainment in the form of a television, video cassette player, drinks dispenser, and a toilet cum wash room. The coach was operated by a driver and steward or stewardess and in 1981 was the last word in modern coach travel.

Pictured at Barnsley bus station outside the Y.T. travel shop, fleet number 64 is a Leyland Leopard with a Plaxton Paramount body which was used for the National Express service to London. Brought into service to supercede the coaches such as number 52, these were built to the same high specification but much higher to give greater luggage capacity and passenger comfort.

Chapter Four

Advertising and Flamboyant Colour Schemes

Buses and trams have been used as mobile bill-boards ever since they started travelling along thoroughfares under public gaze. As coach painting techniques have developed so have the advertisers expanded their imagination to keep pace, resulting in some of the wonderful works of art that can be seen adorning our public transport of today. This chapter illustrates some of the earlier and quite recent attempts of the advertising media to persuade us, the consumers, to purchase their wares.

Pictured in Barnsley bus station this 1950 Roe bodied Leyland Titan PD2/1 is carrying an advertisment for 'Woodbine' the great little cigarette. No health warning here, just two happy looking fellows in flat caps puffing contentedly away. At the side of number 884 can be seen part of 710, a Weymann bodied Guy Arab II.

Again in Barnsley bus station, JHE 829 is a 1956 Leyland Tiger bodied by Roe. The advertising panel is filled with a very eye catching invitation to visit Blackpool for 'Sun-Filled Days and Star-Packed Nights'.

The same position as the previous picture but with subtle differences. The railway signal gantry has grown and a canopy has appeared on the right hand side over the island stands. Here is LHE 511, a Roe bodied Leyland Tiger of 1957 that was rebuilt from Weymann bodied number 751. The advertisment is for 'Sunfresh' fruit drink.

The advertisment for 'Snelsons TV, Radio & Electrical' goods boasting shops in 'Sheffield, Mexbrough, Barnsley, Rotherham, Doncaster' is carried on a 1961 Leyland Titan PD3A/1 with Northern Counties bodywork, here numbered 701, its original number was 1196 until April 1967.

Pictured outside Yorkshire Traction's head office on Sheffield Road, this Daimler Fleetline CRG6LXB with Northern Counties bodywork was purchased from the company and converted into a mobile showroom. Formerly fleet number 640 of 1968 it was taken over by Contractor's Sales of Doncaster Road, Barnsley, and after being converted by Yorkshire Traction engineers was used as a showroom for Calor Gas appliances. The unit would be driven to 'gasless' areas of the district and the local people would be invited on board to see how a Calor Gas cooker or fire could enhance their lives.

This Leyland Atlantean is being used in 1983 as a static display to promote 'Women in the Community', a Women's Institute campaign, outside the British Home Stores in Cheapside, Barnsley.

The bus was sponsored by the National Bus Company and it operated from the Belle Isle depot of the West Riding Bus Company of Wakefield.

Sponsored by Yorkshire Traction Engineering and converted by them into a mobile workshop this Leyland Leopard PSU3B/4R of 1972 is seen outside the Pindar Oaks garage at Upper Sheffield Road, Barnsley. Taken out of service in 1984, fleet number 375 started a new life as a workshop for 'Revup' which was a youth rehabilitation group known as 'The Two Wheel Centre' of Thurnscoe.

Taken in 1983, this picture shows a Bristol VRT/SL2/6LX with E.C.W. bodywork of 1973 in the parking bay at Barnsley bus station. It is advertising National Holidays which could be booked at the Yorkshire Traction Travel Shop located in the bus station. The slogan reads, 'Join the National Holidaymakers' and 'Book at Yorkshire Traction Travel'. This vehicle was the third of a batch of twelve Bristols to swell the ranks of Yorkshire Traction, their fleet numbers being 800 to 811.

Two pictures of the same vehicle in different liveries, firstly commemorating Yorkshire Traction's eightieth birthday in 1982 and secondly promoting Slalom Lager. The bus of many colours is a Bristol VRT/SL2/6LXB of 1975 with an E.C.W. body.

A typical English rainy day – just right for a countryside bus ride! This Leyland National 11351A/1R is parked at the rear of the Sheffield Road maintenance depot. The livery is extolling the virtues of taking a bus ride into the country, even if it is raining. The signwriter's skill can be seen in the use of the 'National' badge as a road sign. At the side can be seen two other National buses in conventional colours.

Pictured during the Yorkshire Traction open day on Sunday 20th April 1980, fleet number 864 has been transformed with a livery dating from 1950's. It is promoting the company's Excusions and Tours and the roundels on the front display 'Skegness' and 'Boulogne-sur-Mer'. 864 is a Bristol VRT/SL3/501 of 1978. Behind can be seen a Leyland Leopard PSU3/4R Weymann bodied coach which is fleet number 14.

A Leyland National MkII of South Yorkshire Transport advertising 'Embassy Window Centres' of Doncaster. Just one of a proliferation of double glazing firms that blossomed in the 1980's.

Promoting 'Panacar Services' this Leyland National 11351A/1R is fleet number 471 and entered service in 1979. The location is just outside Worsbrough village to the south of Barnsley. This in-car entertainment company of Doncaster Road, Kendray, is offering a bewildering array of car radio suppliers and even the front panel of the bus has been used to picture a 'Blaupunkt' radio.

Fleet number 923 is a Bristol VRT/SL3/501 of 1980 with E.C.W. bodywork and is seen advertising the then new Radio Hallam. Proclaiming that it 'Sounds Good 24 Hours A Day' the bus is pictured in Barnsley bus station awaiting some passengers before departing on its route to Doncaster.

This Bristol, number 933, is of the same batch as 923 in the previous photograph and is shown announcing a change of address for a long established Barnsley firm. Eyre Bros. was established in 1927 on Peel Street, in the centre of Barnsley, with an Austin dealership. In 1967 expansion meant a move to Regent Street and then a further move to Huddersfield Road after aquiring a British Leyland franchise. After taking on other makes including Rover, Jaguar and Land-Rover, the final move to Claycliffe Road, Barugh was undertaken. To make sure the public knew of the new location of the firm, the Yorkshire Traction bus was commissioned to very good effect.

Seen in Swinton en route to Kilnhurst this bus is advertising a firm located in Doncaster. Fleet number 922 is, once again, of the same series as the previous two and has been signwritten to promote 'National Travelworld', that was situated in the St. Sepulchre Gate shopping centre in Doncaster.

Photographed on the 18 September 1983, this E.C.W. bodied Leyland Olympian is helping to celebrate eighty years of public service from the Yorkshire Traction Company. The script used is reminiscent of the early years of the company. Number 602 has also carried the same livery as 922 in the previous picture for 'National Travelworld'.

Pictured in a Leeds bus station parking bay in 1984, number 603 is displaying Yorkshire Traction's support for one hundred years of public transport in Huddersfield. The bus, a 1981 Leyland Olympian ONLXB1R with E.C.W. bodywork, has been re-painted in the livery of the County Motors (Lepton) Ltd. of Huddersfield that was bought out by Yorkshire Traction in 1968. Fleet numbers 602 and 603 were both delivered to Yorkshire Traction fitted with electronic destination boards on an experimental basis. They proved to be very unreliable and no more were ordered at this time, crews preferring the tried and tested mechanical units.

Also seen in Leeds this 1983, E.C.W. bodied Leyland Olympian is promoting 'Lion Bitter' from the brewery of Matthew Brown. 'The Pride of the North' could just as well be in praise of the sign writers who so very skillfully hand painted the lion's head on the side of the bus.

Chapter Five

Recovery and Maintenance Vehicles

From the day that motorised transport began running on the public roads they also started to break down and get into various forms of trouble. This led to the development of the 'Recovery Vehicle'; usually, in the beginning a hybrid converted from a redundant bus or lorry but latterly a highly specialised vehicle built to carry out very difficult recovery work. Many smaller contracting vehicles are also utilised for maintenance of buildings and other structures, such as bus stop shelters, that are scattered around the countryside. The Yorkshire Traction Company had a very highly organised maintenance regime centred on Sheffield Road in Barnsley where they could carry out any repair or rebuild to any one of the service vehicles. All other depots had maintenance facilities of varying capacity. This complex also housed the Driver Training Centre which was equipped to prepare drivers for the operation of any of the various types of bus in service at the time.

This A.E.C. Matador recovery vehicles seen parked in the compound of the Yorkshire Traction Bus depot at Wombwell. This vehicle was normally based at the Barnsley depot and despatched to any incident that required the specialist equipment it boasted. Other Y.T. depots maintained converted buses that were used for basic recovery, but any heavy lifting was handled by the major recovery vehicle.

Photographed in 1984 on the Pitfield parking area at Upper Sheffield Road, following its withdrawal, the Matador is enjoying a well earned rest having handed over the heavy recovery duties to its successor, the ex-W.D. Magirus-Deutz.

Pictured in 1979, the Ford Cargo flatbed is awaiting its driver at the rear of the bodyshop in the new Barnsley maintenance depot. This Y.T. company support vehicle was used by the engineering department for the transport of materials around the area. Fitted with both an hydraulic tail lift and Hyab crane this was a very versatile and well used addition to the fleet.

In the right hand background can be seen the vehicle brake test bays under construction, these were made ready for demonstration on the Barnsley depot open day in April 1980. This lower car parking area was for use by staff from the Head Office at Upper Sheffield Road during office hours and for the overnight parking of single deck buses.

The depot manager at this time was Mr. John Methuen and his Triumph 2000 car can be seen to the left of the lorry.

The Magirus Deutz heavy recovery vehicle ready for collection by the Yorkshire Traction engineering department who will undertake its conversion from army to civilian guise, circa 1979. Alongside can be seen a Leyland Atlantean bus freshly painted in the livery of the Mexborough and Swinton bus company.

This vehicle is owned and maintained by the Barnsley Tram and Bus Society who use it for rallies and shows.

Shows the Magirus Deutz after conversion but before painting. The crew are putting the new recovery vehicle through its paces to check out the geometry and effectiveness of the hydraulic lifting gear. An ex London Transport Route Master was borrowed from a firm of dismantlers next door and laid on its side. The new lifting tackle was then deployed and all concerned no doubt held their breath. However, as can be seen, the rig passed its trial with flying colours and was then despatched to the paint shop to receive its smart and flambuoyant livery.

The 'Beast' ready to emerge from the Pindar Oaks cleaning bay at Upper Sheffield Road. Having been converted with the addition of hydraulic lifting gear mounted in the much modified rear portion of the vehicle and a very striking paint job, RV1 is now about to enter service. The new head lights that have been fitted came from a Leyland Olympian bus and the indicator lamps once graced a Bristol VR.

The signwriting promotes a new service offered by the Y.T. company at this time, a twenty four hour recovery service for the general public as well as body repairs and vehicle maintenance.

This bus cleaning bay was high enough to cope with both single and double deck vehicles where they were cleaned and washed inside and out. Having been valetted, the bus would be parked with its entrance door facing one of the hot air blowers mounted on the bay walls and quickly dried out ready for another tour of duty.

Once again, the 'Beast' displays her talents. This time at a Y.T. open day on Sunday 20th April 1980 in front of an audience. The 'casualty' is a driver training bus belonging to the fleet, although the red and white stripes are vertical, where the training livery of Y.T. had them horizontal but all other details are correct. The demonstration is taking place on the Pitfield Parking Area to the rear of the Barnsley Maintenance Depot.

Pictured in 1983 the Yorkshire Traction Engineering utility is parked opposite the garage foreman's office at Pindar Oaks garage. This vehicle covered more miles than any other run by this department and was a regular visitor to a fish and chip shop at Stairfoot whilst collecting the suppers for the night shift staff. Apart from call out to roadside repairs and light recovery, this pickup was regularly used to ferry drivers between depots to ensure that the correct and corresponding number of drivers and buses were present at each one for the start of a shift.

The 1982 Austin Metro van is shown outside the head office on Upper Sheffield Road. The darkly attired gentleman is an inspector, who, with a driver, would travel at random throughout the network checking passenger's tickets and the bus's punctualitty. The inspector would board a bus at a recognised stop and the driver would follow in the van until, having completed his checks, the inspector would alight and be taken to the next route to be surveilled.

The van logo is advertising the Yorkshire Traction Travel Shop.

Seen outside the Barnsley bus station canteen is the Engineering Department's 1980 Ford Transit pickup engaged in some building maintenance work.

To the left is one of the six Leyland Leopard Semi-Coaches which entered service for Yorkshire Traction in 1978/9. Bodied by Plaxtons, these vehicles were used for excursions and local motorway express services.

At the rear of the picture can be seen the old Court House railway offices which are now converted into a public house entitled 'The Court House Station'.

Behind the coach is the only remaining piece of the railway bridge on the approach to the Court House station. This structure still houses the Yorkshire Traction Travel Shop. On the left, towering over everything around, is the Queen's Hotel on Regent Street.

The Yorkshire Traction's other Ford Transit was a 1970 custom van which was used for many years to carry money from the company's different depot cash offices to the main office at Barnsley until a security firm was contracted to perform this task.

The Transit is seen parked outside the Barnsley bus station 'Lost Property Department' and 'Cashing in Office'.

The metamorphosis of a redundant bus into a recovery vehicle in 1983. The first picture shows the bus, fleet number 136, undergoing the first stages of conversion in the body shop at Upper Sheffield Road.

The second shows the vehicle's conversion is well under way. Besides the major bodywork rebuild, the whole chassis and mechanics will receive a thorough overhaul before the final paint finish. All this work will be carried out 'in house' by Yorkshire Traction employees. To the left can be seen fleet number 858, a Bristol VTRSL of 1978, undergoing modifications to rear panels.

The third picture shows the finished vehicle, with a flat bed for carrying goods and a self contained workshop behind the cab, at its place of work, the Waterloo depot at Huddersfield. This building was formerly home to twenty-three buses of 'County Motors', taken over by Yorkshire Traction in 1968.

COME HOME TO A REAL FIRE
YORKSHIRE TRACTION
21

YORKSHIRE TRACTION a NATIONAL bus company
RECOVERY
L9
270 RA
YORKSHIRE TRACTION
Engineering

Pictured in 1984 at the Pitfield parking area at the rear of the maintenance depot in Upper Sheffield Road, is one of two Leyland Buffalo recovery vehicles that were owned by Yorkshire Traction at this time. Specially built for the job they were originally numbered L2 and L5 until the arrival of the 'Beast' when they were re-titled RV2 and RV3 respectively following on from the larger vehicle which was numbered RV1.

Also photographed in 1984 is L2, the other Leyland Buffalo recovery vehicle is posing in the lower car parking area behind the paint shop and bodyshop at Upper Sheffield Road. Standng in front of the vehicle to the right is Mr. Alan Lawton, a foreman fitter with the Yorkshire Traction Engineering department.

Seen parked at the main entrance to the head office at Upper Sheffield Road alongside the Pindar Oaks garage is Leyland Buffalo L5. Standing to the side is one of the Leyland Leopard semi-coaches that has just re-fuelled before returning to work on the local motorway express service.

To the right in the picture can be seen a stone detached building that was used as the traffic department offices. Now sadly demolished, the space was earmarked for future development of the headquarters. Above the headboard of the recovery vehicle can be seen the empty hole where a clock was situated for use by road staff checking the departure times of vehicles going into service.

Awaiting repair in the Pitfield parking area is a Leyland National Mk.1 B52F of 1979. It was damaged after skidding on ice in the winter of 1984 whilst on a colliery works service. In this instance, swift repairs were carried out and number 482 was quickly back in service.

Leyland National Mk.1 of 1973, fleet number 411, displays the result of an incident involving some other vehicle during 1984 and is awaiting attention at the Pitfield parking area. Number 411 was among the first fifteen Mk.1's to enter service with Yorkshire Traction in 1973. An additional two were purchased in 1973 and no less than eighty-three arrived between 1976/9 making the total up to one hundred, numbers 400 to 499.

Ravaged by fire, this Bristol VRTSL number 862 was introduced into the Yorkshire Traction fleet along with thirty others between 1976 and 1978. These were numbered from 833 to 864. The damage seen here was thought to have been caused by children on the upper deck rear seats.

The vehicle carries the 'MetroBus' insignia for operations in the West Yorkshire areas.

Doncaster-London
£6 SINGLE
£7.50 DAY RETURN
NATIONAL EXPRESS
HWJ 924W
924
BRISTOL VR

Number 924, a Bristol VRTSL of 1981, suffered servere damage to its roof whilst being transferred from Doncaster to Wombwell depot at night in readiness for the next day's work. The driver, used to operating single-decker buses, forgot that this time he was in charge of a double-decker and attempted to negotiate a low bridge with disastrous results. However, a piece of smart thinking by the Engineering Department gave the Yorkshire Traction an opportunity to acquire an open-top bus for festive and corporate occasions. Further ingenuity enabled the vehicle to become a convertible with a removeable hard-top. The lifting eyes for the roof can be seen on the third picture which shows the hard-top in position.

These pictures, taken in March 2000, show the replacement for the Magirus Deutz which has taken the fleet number RV1. A Bristol VRTSL, it started life as fleet number 800 in 1973 as the first Bristol double deck vehicle to join Yorkshire Traction. In the mid eighties it was transferred to the driver training unit and became number T2. Now, after having heavy towing gear fitted and the top deck removed to ensure its passage anywhere on the network, including all low bridges, it takes on a new lease of life as the number one recovery vehicle. Inside the lower deck are crew's quarters and a fully fitted workshop.

Yorkshire Traction operated several training vehicles of both single and double deck that were used for driver assessment prior to being employed and for on-going training of experienced operatives.

This Leyland Titan PD3/4 with northern Counties body was supplied to the Southdown fleet in 1967 and was transferred to Yorkshire Traction in 1979 and operates as T6. This vehicle has a four speed manual gearbox and is used to upgrade drivers to a full PSV licence covering manual and automatic gearchanging.

In the background can be seen the old Central Workshop that is capable of accommodating seven vehicles and carrying out all major mechanical maintenance.

T4 is Leyland Leopard PSU3/4R of 1967 with Marshall bodywork. When this bus was in service its fleet number was 220. The picture was taken in 1983 at Wombwell depot.

Having just had a wash and brush-up T7, a Leyland Leopard PSU3B/4R with an Alexander body, is ready to carry on with training duties. The former fleet number was 135.

A large part of the training was familiarisation with routes and the different bus stations the new drivers would have to negotiate whilst at work. It has been said that the best lunches were to be had at the Dewsbury bus station and the times were few and far between when a Yorkshire Traction training vehicle was not parked up at Dewsbury during the lunch period.

Pictured in 1983 outside the central workshops at Upper Sheffield Road, this Leyland National Mk1 of 1973 has been given the number T1 in place of fleet number 400. Compared to the Leopard T7 this vehicle was very pleasant to drive, its only drawback being a tendency to roll on corners.

This double-decker, a Bristol VRTSL6G with ECW body, is used for testing trainees when they obtain their PSV licences which covers both single and double-decker buses. This now suffices for the majority of drivers as Yorkshire Traction only own two vehicles that do not have automatic gearboxes and to drive these a further test must be taken on T6. When part of the service fleet this bus ran under the number 800.

Formerly fleet number 801, this Bristol was next in line to T2 and was used as a back up vehicle when there was a backlog of driver testing to be done. Earlier in its career this bus had been converted to power steering by the Yorkshire Traction Engineering Department, but it hardly ever worked properly. In consequence drivers were constantly complaining about the very heavy steering and how they could not manoeuvre it around corners. Then one night a twelve-year old boy got into the parking area at Upper Sheffield Road and drove T10 round one of the tightest corners in the compound before abandoning it. Thereafter no driver had the nerve to complain again.

Chapter Six

The Development of Barnsley Bus Station

Starting as a line of 'stands' in Eldon Street for the early trams, the 'terminus' expanded rapidly and by 1936 the bus operators were using starting stands in Kendray Street, Midland Street, Church Street, Doncaster Road, Peel Street and Gas Nook.

Barnsley needed a bus station very urgently, and in October 1936 a site was earmarked for the first purpose built terminus adjacent to the London, Midland and Scottish Railway's Barnsley Exchange Station on the lower level and the viaduct of the Court House Station served formerly by the Midland Railway. William Johnson & Son of Park Street, Wombwell were the contractors who started work on the 27th October 1937 and brought the contract to a successful conclusion on Wednesday 13 December 1938 when Barnsley's new Omnibus Station was opened.

Four platforms, A,B,C and D, linked by safety crossings, to enable passengers to move freely without danger, were to cater for up to 3,000 arrivals and departures a day. Yorkshire Traction's General Manager, Mr G.W. Robinson, was very proud of the bus station's toilet facilities where hot running water was available in the ladies room. The catering facilities were franchised to Godley's, whose cafe was capable of seating one hundred diners for anything between a sandwich and a hot meal.

Two newspaper kiosks were established, one, located on the Centre Island, was known as the 'threepenny bit' and was extensively used as a rendezvous for young lovers. The other, having only half the number of sides, was aptly christened the 'three ha'pence'.

This station survived until the 1970's without major alteration but was then completely re-built to last until the turn of the century when it is once again undergoing a great deal of change.

Taken from the entrance to the Exchange railway station at the junction of Eldon Street and Regent Street, this photograph shows the recently cleared site ready for construction work to begin. The London Midland and Scottish Railway ran behind the wall at the top of the picture, where a signal gantry can be seen and further to the right the footbridge that crossed Queens Road is just visible. The pole finial in the bottom right of the picture is a relic of the tram era and the arm seen to the left of the L.M.S sign board once supported the trolley wire.

Showing the new covered stands in the course of construction along the boundary wall with the L.M.S. railway line. All the parapernalia of a building site can be seen cluttering the newly laid concrete roadway. The C.E.A.G. building at the rear to the right of the picture is shown under construction on the site of a former fellmonger's premises that burnt down in 1935. The manufacturers of mining, vehicle and industrial lighting have occupied this well known Barnsley landmark since moving from Regent Street in 1936. The row of terraced houses in front of this structure was soon to be demolished and the site used for the storage of coal transported by the railway awaiting local distribution by coal-merchants. The buildings to the left also disappeared in the quest for modernisation to be replaced with the Granada Bingo Hall and the once renowned 'Ba Ba' Club, owned by the versatile and entertaining stage hypnotist, the late Peter Casson.

Taken from the same position some months later, this photograph shows the central stand well on the way to completion. The walls at both ends of the site have now been demolished to allow access to the bus station. The covered stands at each side have been finished and the administration block to the left is shortly to receive its roof.

After completion the administration block, shown to the left in the previous pictue, served the bus station well through the years as can be seen from this photograph taken in 1983 but since demolished in 1999. Access through the centre door led to subterranean toilets with staff canteen above to the left and inspector's canteen and time office to the right. The low brick building to the right was the Lost Property Department and also housed the union office. (TGWU).

Pictured shortly after completion, the new bus station is shown to be very busy with all stands in use and a great number of buses and coaches jostling for position. There does not appear to be any 'Rule of the Road' with regard to one way working, it seems to be a complete free for all and some of the traffic jams must have been wonderous to behold. The stand on the right is very busy with people both coming and going, as is the centre stand. The buses in the picture, numbering about thirty, are a diverse variety of makes, models and liveries demonstrating the wide range of vehicles that were in use during this period.

The same scene today. Still prominent is the C.E.A.G. building and to the far left, in the background, is the Bingo Hall. In the foreground is part of the Courthouse car park and a small section of the original wall is preserved. To the right can be seen the remains of the abutment that supported the bridge carrying the L.N.E.R. metals over Eldon Street and the L.M.S. line before entering the Courthouse Station.

Shown in the late 1950's this Brush bodied Dennis Lancet 111, fleet number 856, is loading passengers at stand number 13 and will leave in the direction of Kendray Street and Queens Road on the route to Worsbrough Bridge. To the right can be seen the 'Threepenny Bit' newsagent's kiosk so beloved as a rendezvous point at this time.

Three pictures of exactly the same location, stand 30, taken over some twelve years. The first shows a 1958 Leyland Tiger Cub PSUC1/1 with Park Royal body waiting below a newly painted sign. The second picture displays the painted number having suffered the ravages of time, although everything else seems to have survived without much change. The third photograph depicts a 1968 Leyland Atlantean PDR1/3 with Northern Counties bodywork leaving the bus station with stand 30 behind. The Almond's bakery van is delivering the bread and cakes for the station restaurant situated close by. The more modern vehicle is a 1970 Daimler Fleetline SRG6LX with a Marshall body. This bus was used mainly for the Motorway Express Service between Leeds and Mexborough.

ATHERSLEY STH CIRCULAR
0 6
IONDS
YORKSHIRE TRACTIO
652
NHE 52F
YORKSHIRE TRACTION

Taken in the mid 1950s this picture shows a 1951 Leyland Titan PD2/1 standing in the bus station with the Queen's Hotel behind to the left. On the far right can be seen the railway bridge crossing Eldon Street where the railway entered the Court House station. The structure is at this time still complete and proudly carries an advertisment for the local 'Oakwell Brewery'.

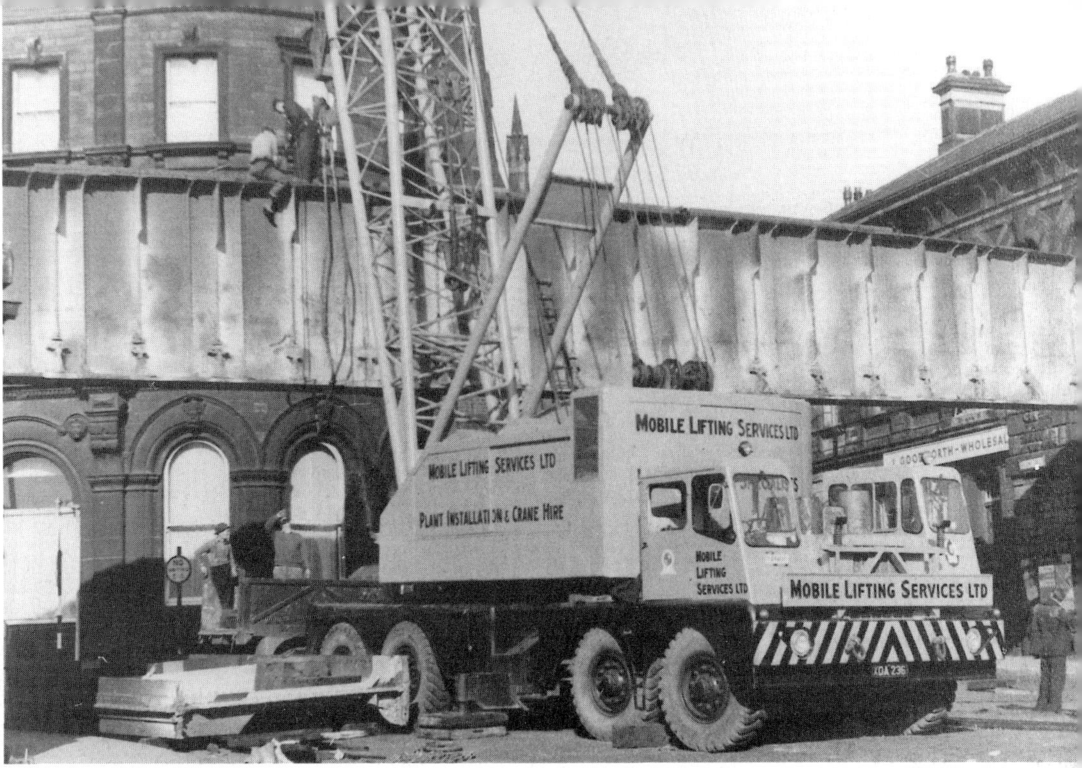

Following the closure of the Court House Station on the 15th April 1960, the rails were lifted and this photograph shows the bridge over Eldon Street being dismantled. Behind, to the left is the Queen's Hotel and right, the Court House Building. A part of the railway bridge arches and abutments are preserved today as listed buildings one of which houses the Yorkshire Traction travel and information centre.

The remainder of the railway bridge as it is preserved today clearly showing the abutment where the steel girders rested before being removed. This picture, taken in March 2000, shows the bus station undergoing yet another metamorphosis. The Yorkshire Traction Travel Link and Infolink are still intact with the original canopy in situ. To the left is the large block of shops built in Midland Street on the site of the bridge that carried the rails into the Court House Station.

In the early 1970's a lot of re-development was taking place in Barnsley town centre and the bus station did not escape. Here can be seen the demolition of a further part of the Midland Railway high level viaduct which ran along the length of Midland Street. The faced building to the left contained the bus station cafe where one could always buy an 'Albert Hurst Pie' to be served with mushy peas. This item was top of the menu for many years.

Further demolition and clearance work taking place along the line of the high level viaduct. To the right is the site of the former cafe seen in the previous picture. This area was developed as part of the new market complex and the Barnsley Council offices. The Civic Hall can be seen together with the jewellers shop, Benjamin Harold with its prominent clock overhanging the pavement.

Taken from the Jumble Lane level crossing looking towards the new Midland Street parade of shops under construction. The centre stand of the bus station is still in use despite the building work. The town hall clock can just be seen on the extreme left of the picture with the Odeon cinema to the centre. The spire belonged to the Congregational Church which is now demolished. On the far right is the Queen's Hotel situated on the corner of Eldon street and Regent Street opposite the main entrance to the bus station.

Pictured in the early 1970's, this 1962 Willowbrook bodied Leyland Leopard is parked in the overspill park at the rear of the Exchange Railway Station with the Queen's Hotel and the old Court House building behind.

The same view taken in 2000 showing the latest developments of this part of the bus station. The Eastern Counties Leyland Olympian is awaiting passengers in what is now the North Bus Station with the Barnsley Interchange to the rear. Still unchanged are the Queens Hotel and The Old Court House.

Pictured in the late 1980s, Jumble Lane crossing is suffering the removal of its footbridge which was considered redundant due to the proposed installation of traffic lights and new automatic barriers. The coal merchant's yard can be clearly seen between the railway and the Granada Bingo building. The signal box to the left of the crossing was, of course, entitled 'Jumble Lane Crossing'.

The same view as the previous photograph but taken in 2000. Not a lot has changed. The bingo hall is now run by Gala, the level crossing is fully automated and the signal box has been fitted with replacement window frames. The main development is the transformation of the coal yard into the Barnsley East bus station which is now linked into one large transport interchange between road and rail.

INDEX TO BARNSLEY BUSES